THE Perfect COUNTRY ROOM

THE Perfect COUNTRY ROOM

EMMA-LOUISE O'REILLY

Conran Octopus

First published in 1996 by
Conran Octopus Limited
37 Shelton Street
London WC2H 9HN

ISBN 1-85029-865-3

Commissioning Editor: Suzannah Gough
Senior Editor: Jenna Jarman
Editorial Assistant: Helen Woodhall
Copy Editor: Sarah Sears

Art Editor: Karen Bowen
Picture Researcher: Julia Pashley

Production Controller: Mano Mylvaganam
Indexer: Indexing Specialists

British Library Cataloguing-in-Publication
Data
A catalogue record for this book is available
from the British Library

Printed in Hong Kong

Contents

INTRODUCTION

We ALL THINK WE KNOW WHAT THE PERFECT COUNTRY ROOM SHOULD BE LIKE. A SERIES OF GENTLE IMAGES DANCES BEFORE OUR EYES IN DAYDREAMING MOMENTS. THERE IS MORE URGENCY TODAY IN THE LONGING FOR THE REALIZATION OF THIS IDYLL BECAUSE OF THE RAPIDITY WITH WHICH UNSPOILT COUNTRYSIDE IS BEING EATEN UP BY UNSYMPATHETIC DEVELOPMENT. SO WE DREAM OF THE PERFECT RETREAT, SEEMINGLY FAR FROM THE PRESSURES OF MODERN LIVING, WHERE WE CAN ATTEMPT TO LIVE A MORE PEACEFUL LIFE.

LEFT

A bed in a hut in a landscape – the perfect country room connects with its setting in new and imaginative ways. Individuality and a lightness of touch are its hallmarks.

ABOVE *Stripped of ornament and empty of furniture, the architecture and space of a hallway take on new interest, and the simple designs of ordinary details like mouldings, door hinges and handles are revealed.*

ABOVE RIGHT *In imitation of a stately enfilade with its glimpses of gilded furniture and pictures, this sequence of rooms has a more light-hearted character with its hot, bright colours and modern furniture.*

FAR RIGHT *The matt finish of new paintwork is juxtaposed with the battered surfaces of an old sideboard. Rich yellow and grey-brown walls provide an unusual and sympathetic backdrop for its simple, generous design.*

*T*here is no shortage of ideas on how to create the perfect country retreat; it is a rich seam of design, philosophy and tradition which has been mined in every generation to produce a new interpretation. From the Roman villas on the Bay of Naples to the converted farmhouses of New England and the woodland cabins of today's romantic spirits, country interiors have tried to combine an atmosphere of informality with differing measures of comfort and the joys of life in the country.

In our own century the Arts and Crafts Movement represented a purposeful revisiting of rural building traditions, at the same time that labourers' cottages were being bought up by the middle classes and an appropriate country look was being sought to furnish them. Since then, these two directions have been strong themes in the history of country interiors. Although it is easy to laugh at the quaintness of supposedly appropriate rustic interiors of the 1920s, the subjectiveness of taste and the speed with which it changes makes this inevitable. In the 1950s and 1960s, a specifically English country house look evolved – influencing taste on both sides of the Atlantic – in which well-behaved arrangements of good furniture and pictures looked quietly elegant in a sort of *en tout cas* 'Georgian' interior. The discipline of this look gradually relaxed its grip as more and more people began to grow confident about expressing their personalities in their interior decoration.

'With the sure touch of a stage manager, associations and evocations of different styles and atmospheres are deftly made, while a discerning eye enjoys the good honest design of simple things alongside well chosen antiques.'

LEFT *In a converted Irish schoolhouse, a living room draws on grand, country house drawing room layouts to furnish a lofty space. The proportions make this solution plausible and the simple architecture and humbler detailing loosen the formality traditional in such rooms. The elegant pictures hung on the fireplace wall are convincingly aristocratic, but if the eye travels up into the roof space it is apparent that no effort has been made to continue the theme. This lightness of touch is also apparent in the easy way in which two ordinary kitchen chairs fit into the scheme.*

RIGHT *Unfussy cottage furnishings sit quietly in a determinedly simple room. The only unexpected drama comes with the generous draping of a high-backed settle.*

*A*s a result of wider travel and greater access to all sorts of inspirational sources, there has been a tremendous appetite for country things in the last twenty years and in response country interiors have been decorated and redecorated a hundred times, with endless textile ranges being dedicated to the 'country look', kitchen designs conceived around it, and furniture built for it. More recently, it seemed that the country cottage was in danger of disappearing in clouds of flowery fabrics and hedges of dried herbs. Between the clichés of traditional country interiors and the new country products being marketed, the vision of a simpler life seemed to have become blurred. The country cottage had become like the aged actress who wears so much rouge that it is impossible to make out the dear old features.

So things have begun to swing back the other way, and along the route new ideas have been incorporated in sparer country interiors. Most importantly, it is now the architecture of the house or converted barn or water tower that sets the pace, and its history, its setting and its individuality are much more often the cue for the decoration of the interior than this or that 'look'. The dignity of the architecture is paramount however humble the building and whatever new building work is carried out. The personality of the owner expressed in the evidence of particular hobbies or interests and in collections of books or pictures is then threaded through the house to create a new and individual synthesis of ideas in the interior.

Perfect
SETTINGS

*T*O FIND A LITTLE CORNER OF UNSPOILT COUNTRYSIDE WHERE THE AIR IS GOOD, THE EARTH

IS FERTILE AND THE VIEWS UNBROKEN, IS TO FIND A LITTLE PIECE OF HEAVEN ON EARTH. THE

PERFECT SETTING FOR A HOME IN THE COUNTRY IS SO OFTEN, IT SEEMS, 'AT THE END OF A

CART TRACK', WHETHER IT IS UP A MOUNTAIN OR DOWN A SECRET VALLEY, BY A FLAT

MIRROR OF A LAKE OR ON A LONELY HEADLAND SURROUNDED ON THREE SIDES BY THE SEA,

WITH THE WAVES CRASHING ON THE SHORE.

LEFT AND ABOVE
*Wedged between rocks, with the biggest
views of sky and sea, this cottage promises
refuge in a dramatic setting. The gable
decoration above mimics a dinghy's hull.*

LEFT *A tower for a modern-day Rapunzel on an Italian hillside; its rugged construction looks as if it has been thrown up by its stony landscape. Roof tiles and cypresses dent the summer sky; shutters are thrown open to air the cool, dark interior.*

BELOW *In the heat of the afternoon the only shade is cast by the whirling shape of a bell frame on this brilliant white wall.*

BOTTOM *The warm colours of terracotta air bricks are combined in a framed design of diamonds and squares.*

RIGHT *Golden broom shimmers around the ankles of a sturdy Umbrian farmhouse. Its jumble of roof pitches makes no concessions to symmetry or prettiness.*

A garden can be created and a house can be turned upside down but the setting is God-given, and though man might have the temerity to intervene here and there, the matter is really out of his hands. An element of happy chance rather than design makes a house in a perfect setting all the more precious.

The relationship between the house and this precious setting is an intimate one: the house is not an independent box of treasures but is tied to its landscape by the materials in which it is built. The local stone, locally made bricks, timber, roof tiles, shingles or slates of its construction give it a sense of place. Blending in colour and texture with its setting, it takes up its position on the spur of a hill or a bend in the river as if it had always been there.

'Blending with its
setting, a house takes
up its position on
the spur of a hill or
a bend in the river as
if it had always
been there.**'**

LEFT *Peace and calm hang in the air
around this Texan farmhouse surrounded by
oak and elm trees, a herb garden and flower
beds. Built by German settlers, it is
substantial but not grand, and its long,
shady verandah and widely spaced windows
give it an open, welcoming aspect. The
gentle landscape setting with its mirror of
a pond bordered by weeping willows makes
it an idyllic spot.*

LEFT *The grandeur of crags and peaks makes a human dwelling seem tiny and fragile but in fact a mountain chalet needs to be of sturdy design. Built using local stone and timber, the overhanging eaves and chimneys, log stores and enclosing walls of this building all hint at a way of life that is dictated by its isolation.*

RIGHT *A childhood dream comes true in the building of this ultimate refuge: a wooden tree house with a biblical-looking ladder, a balcony, a proper pitched roof and windows. Going back to nature takes on a new dimension. An occasional feature of adventure stories and children's tales, the idea of living in a tree must spring from some atavistic longing. As dawn breaks and the sun comes up, there is no-one around but the birds and the wind in the branches.*

'A hideaway built out of the landscape to which it will one day return brings back childhood memories; here one can be close to nature and refresh the spirits.'

Others would find it easier to recharge their batteries in a house in the middle of a rolling plain, big skies and endless open spaces lying outside their door. At night you can look up and feel you have a ringside view of the heavens. The building will probably be long and low, blending with the flat landscape; and the interior, which cannot hope to echo the great spaces outdoors, will be simple and comfortable.

Far from the endless landlocked plain are the fishermen's houses and coast guards' cottages on a rocky coastline. A house here may seem built into the rock which embraces and shelters it. It has views only out to sea, for its back windows look out onto the dark and craggy cliff. Fishing villages built in a natural amphitheatre around a little bay are amongst the most picturesque of settings – whether soaking up the sun in the Mediterranean or coping with storms in a more northern climate. When these houses were built rough seas spelt only danger for their inhabitants, but the romantic appeal of the sea in all its moods means that for some it is the only perfect setting. Houses in the dunes of Jutland in Denmark, on the shores of Maine or on a bleak pebble spit stretching out to sea all take a beating from the elements, and both exterior and interior express the toughness they need to withstand the storms. Previous generations may well not have built where people want to live now, so often houses in these exposed settings are early twentieth-century cabins, or even new houses.

Grander country houses, on the other hand, in their own tailored landscape, and farms with their land around them were always more aloof and often self-sufficient. The appeal of a self-sufficient holding is as old as history. How many people long to live on their own land, to grow a few vegetables, to have a little orchard, some chickens and beehives? How many frustrated city dwellers dream of a peaceful life in a setting like this? An Italian *casa colonica* in the rolling Umbrian hills bordered by its olive trees and a vineyard, an English Cotswold house nestled in a verdant valley with its walled garden, neat rows of vegetables and espaliered fruit trees, a Greek farmhouse with beehives nearby: each is in its way perfect and offers the opportunity of living in true harmony with nature and enjoying the careful husbandry of the land which has been worked by generation after generation.

LEFT AND ABOVE
*A walled garden sits in a gentle landscape and a
cottage door emerges from behind the glorious
colours of an English garden in summer.*

LEFT *More than any other building, a log cabin seems a part of its landscape. It is the perfect house in the woods: simple architecture blends with its surroundings, promising the cosy picturebook homeliness of a gingerbread house. Those searching for peace nowadays find its simplicity is its biggest attraction, and straightforward building design and local materials are also part of this appeal.*

RIGHT *This gothic hut is an eye-catcher at the end of a meadow walk; rather than blending into its setting it stands out boldly against a woodland backdrop. A simple wooden cabin, it has been transformed into a picturesque and striking garden building – with its pointed arches, door surround and trefoil window picked out in black. Perhaps it is the perfect retreat for the writer, a private little world probably furnished with inspirational talismans and a favourite armchair. No-one might enter without an invitation and no-one knows how much hard work and how much solitary daydreaming goes on here.*

*A*lthough the joys of a pastoral life away from worldly cares have been celebrated in many traditions by poets, statesmen and kings, there were only ever a few people who could afford the luxury of a purpose-built villa or country retreat. From the Roman villas of Capri to the *faux*-rustique inventions of the eighteenth-century European aristocracies and the lodges of American industrialists and bankers in the Adirondacks or along the east coast, there have been attempts, at times of prosperity in every age, to try and capture the elusive rural idyll in new intepretations reflecting the preoccupations of the time. But it was not until the end of the last century that the labourer's cottage became an object of delight for the professional classes wanting to get away from it all to a simple rural setting. The English love affair with cottage architecture had gathered momentum during the nineteenth century with variable results, and it quickly turned into a headlong dash for every tumbledown country cottage within reasonable distance of the big cities.

'*A farmhouse with its barns and farmyard may differ in style from one region to another, but each shares its history with the landscape in which it sits.*'

*A*t this time the Arts and Crafts Movement, which specifically revisited and treasured a vernacular rural tradition in Britain, America and Germany, was reinventing 'simple' though often substantial perfect country homes. This was probably the last burst of country building activity, in England anyway, when a lack of planning controls allowed great choice of setting.

Recently a quiet rebellion has taken place against the idea of the obvious big country houses, the conventional polite manors and farmhouses, plantation houses and rectories furnished with suitable antiques, in favour of simpler and sometimes quirkier homes. There is a new interest in creating country interiors in unconventional spaces, which might be anything from the clever conversion into several homes of a very large country house or the conversion of redundant rural industrial buildings, mills, water towers, pumping stations and railway stations which have all found new lives as homes. Their settings tell their histories and give a hint of what their interiors might reveal: mills standing by rivers, railway stations on closed lines, boathouses on lakes. For those prepared to go one step further, and who do not want to be tied down by the permanence of bricks and mortar, the only answer is a treehouse, a caravan or a railway carriage parked in a field, huts and cabins, where the great outdoors is the living room. These homes celebrate spontaneity, a string of picnics and the simplest of simple lives. Pared-down country living like this, in the perfect setting, is an uncompromising new departure which many more long for but few achieve.

FAR LEFT *The colours of the weathered timbers of this building soften its lines and give it character. From silvery whites to dark browns, the knots and striations create strange and beautiful patterns across the surface of its walls.*

LEFT *Rugged stone slabs are used as steps outside this Norwegian shepherd's house. A porch with carved detailing provides a shelter from which to watch the surrounding fields and there is no garden or enclosure to separate the house from its landscape.*

ABOVE *Crude classical detailing has been applied here to a simple wooden house in a snowy Scandinavian landscape. Borrowing selectively from the classical tradition, the builders of this house have ended up with a provincial interpretation, whose detailing has been picked out in different colours.*

Perfect
LIVING ROOMS

*T*HE COUNTRY LIVING ROOM NEEDS TO BE A VERSATILE, PRACTICAL SETTING FOR ALL SORTS

OF ACTIVITIES, PROVIDING A SERENE BACKDROP FOR READING OR WRITING IN COMFORT,

MUSIC-MAKING, TÊTE-À-TÊTE CONVERSATION, PARTIES – PERHAPS DANCING – AND CHILDREN

PLAYING. IT NEEDS TO WORK AS WELL BY NIGHT AS IT DOES BY DAY. THE MANY DEMANDS

MADE UPON IT ARE BEING MET TODAY BY INCREASINGLY IMAGINATIVE AND IDIOSYNCRATIC

SCHEMES WHICH TAKE THEIR CUE FROM A WIDE RANGE OF SOURCES.

LEFT
*Garden furniture mimics a formal living room
arrangement in a dark wood-panelled setting
and instead of pictures on the wall there are
draughtsboards and fishing trophies.*

*T*he best country living rooms seem to be those where a mutual respect is evident between owner and house, and where people seem to have listened to their house to discover what it wanted before they embarked on redecorating it. The result is a personal synthesis of ideas and elements which are creative and inspirational. And it is in the living room – perhaps of all the rooms in the house the one most given over to enjoyment and the pleasures of life – that the opportunities are greatest for fun, wit and quiet elegance.

As elsewhere in the house, it is the architecture which tells the story of the room and sets the tone for the decorative scheme. In a cottage or old farm there may well not have been a 'parlour' before, so the room may have changed its function, windows may have been blocked up, there may be a stone door lintel inexplicably jutting out of a wall. Conversions of rural industrial or redundant farm buildings are full of these oddities and enjoying them, or at least not covering them up, is seen today as a mark of respect to the house. There are many ways of drawing the architecture into a decorative scheme: by focusing on the materials of the building – whether rough-finished door planks or stone window mouldings; by introducing or making use of architectural 'furniture' like window seats; by not crowding the room with furniture or smothering the floor space with rugs. In sympathy with this approach there has recently been a reaction against tricksy wall treatments and busy wallpapers in favour of texture: bare, even unplastered walls, or strong smoky colours and traditional paints. So much country building is straightforward – if not humble – that dignity is its main virtue, and if that dignity is compromised by superficial showiness or by too many possessions, it loses its appeal.

FAR LEFT *A quiet corner, a favourite chair and a book hold the promise of a peaceful afternoon. Comfortable furniture is set against the simplest of architecture, where the bones of the building are an essential part of the decorative scheme. The colours, patterns and texture of an ancient panelled wall and door need no further ornamentation.*

LEFT *A scheme of blues in this Swedish living room engages the eye, from the weave of a rug to a bunch of candles hanging on a hook. The sophisticated detailing of the day bed provides a striking contrast with the unabashed plainness of the rest of the room.*

ABOVE *A traditional fireplace design is a reminder of the house's setting and always gives a living room a sense of place and history. Old-fashioned bellows, wrought iron pokers and tongs are as decorative as they are practical.*

LEFT *In this farm–building conversion the end wall has been replaced by glass, emphasizing the spaciousness of the room which needs the oversized tables and sofa to complement it. The collection of bottles displayed on a table is tightly grouped in a disciplined contained area; they make a stronger impression like this than if they were dotted about on every surface.*

RIGHT *The restrained elegance of an historic interior extends to the choice and layout of modern and antique furniture. A playful note is struck by the farm ladder which leans up against the wall, urging us not to take the sophistication too seriously.*

*T*he same restraint applies to newly built country living rooms and new work in converted barns. The tendency today is for simple interiors, where light and space are more of a priority than decorative features for their own sake. In a new building in the country local materials like stone and wood are used baldly and boldly as structure and decoration. Wooden roof structures zigzag across lofty spaces and suspended sleeping platforms provide occasional ceilings down the length of an opened-up barn-house. Walls are likely to be plastered and washed with a single colour, perhaps a bright one in a warmer climate, so that the eye can follow their shapes right up into the roof. Little bites of colour are missing where the roof joists meet them, so that each wall looks like a piece of a jigsaw. Where rooms are lined with tongue and groove panelling the planks and joints provide texture and pattern so that nothing more elaborate is needed as decoration, except perhaps pictures or furniture set against them.

In a small cottage it often seems that everything about it is perfect, except that it lacks just one sizeable room as the living room. One spacious room can open up a house; larger furniture which it would be difficult to accommodate elsewhere can be used, and the room can have a drama and interest quite different from the other rooms however attractive they might be in their own way. A sizeable living room is most often achieved in a smaller house by knocking through walls on the ground floor, or sometimes by building on an extension in the spirit of the old house.

In England, from the time at the end of the last century when country house living was becoming more informal and the country 'look' was becoming more homely, country house work for architects might include adding relatively low-ceilinged but

*'If grand things
can feel at ease
in small living rooms,
so too can humble
things sit happily in
more formal rooms.'*

otherwise generously proportioned informal living rooms to older houses where rooms were deemed too small and where ground plans could not adapt themselves to modern requirements. These extensions were executed with great flair using the same materials and similar proportions in all the details of windows, doors and other internal joinery as the rest of the house, so that they blended in discreetly. Unlike a modern house built all of a piece, an extension needs to spell out its links with the old building and to defer to it, whilst establishing its own identity in the spaciousness of its design and proportions.

Perhaps nothing is more important to a living room than space and airiness – a recurrent theme in the search for the perfect interior not only in the recently popularized Scandinavian interiors but in the Arts and Crafts interiors of Britain and elsewhere from the beginning of this century. Space creates a restfulness not only

LEFT *A deeply comfortable sofa makes any living room perfect. It makes no concession to daintiness, dominating a small room, but its friendly profile is a welcoming sight. Here a traditional English living room follows a conventional path with layers of rugs and an old-fashioned pelmet over the window. Unfussy and relaxed, this room is quite modest in scale but successfully combines a civilized level of comfort with the proportions of a simple cottage room.*

RIGHT *A room of contrasts, with a nineteenth-century sofa made for a rather more bourgeois setting than it now enjoys. A rough stone floor and the exposed workings of a timber and tile roof contain a living room which hovers between outdoors and indoors – with double doors opening directly onto a courtyard. No amount of pictures or ornament would be able to disguise the rugged character of the room which is complemented by country ceramics, a painted cupboard and a chunky table, but the blue and cream striped silk upholstery and the polished arms of the sofa are a sophisticated foil to it.*

LEFT *Wood is used in three different ways in a corner of a living room: roughly chopped as logs for fuel, hewn into chunky structural timbers and fashioned into the solid designs of country furniture. The colour and patterns of wood always provide decorative interest.*

RIGHT *A fireplace that draws well is perhaps the most important element in any successful living room. Here, in an unconventional twist, the vases on the mantelpiece have been placed as if they were samples in a showroom. A sure eye has collected and arranged them to display their graduating shades of milky colours in an orderly parade which also allows appreciation of their individual designs.*

for the mind but also for the eye. Space around a piece of furniture makes it easier to appreciate; it hints at the world outdoors and the surrounding countryside; and space and fewer possessions make the room more practical. Space is the greatest luxury too – the invisible expense – particularly in a small country like England, where old cottages stand on plots which are tiny in comparison to the spacious homesteads and open landscapes of north America.

Where an old house is being put in order – and a change in layout is appropriate – or where a new house is being built, the creation of the right space is the key to making a room work successfully. If it is only practical to create one spacious room, the living room probably takes priority over the remodelling of other rooms because of the need to make visitors and family feel at ease in a well thought-out space attuned to today's way of life. Compromises made over the shape and proportions of a room are of course the most difficult to reverse whereas decoration, and the arrangement of furniture, books and ornaments can be finalized gradually.

Where this is not possible and the rooms are tiny, there is perhaps even more need to create the impression of space by including very few pieces of furniture and little in the way of decorative detail that would distract the eye from any architectural character the room possesses. Another solution is to go in the opposite direction and to treat the room as if it were a *Wunderkammer*, a little cabinet of treasures, filling it with closely hung pictures, books and interesting ornaments, thereby creating the impression that it is a private little corner of a larger room.

'The fireplace or stove as a focal point is the still centre of this turning world and is recognized as an icon of home and warmth everywhere.'

RIGHT *The warm browns and pinks of bare brickwork and a plain wood mantelshelf dominate this interior but there are signs of more sophisticated tastes: in the elaborate fireback which has come from a grander fireplace, and in books and satiricul prints scattered around the room. Intellectual interests are represented in a personal interpretation of the simple life.*

FAR RIGHT *The barest cottage interior appeals to those with ascetic tastes, who long to do away with the soft furnishings of a traditional living room, electric lighting and other mod cons. A room like this, lit with candles and warmed by a roaring fire, is as far from modern cosseting as you can get. Yet the comforts it does offer are enough to make living with the bare but romantic essentials an enjoyable experience.*

other end of the scale there seems to be a determined – almost savage – break with the traditions of a living room, which leaves links with the past hanging by a thread as a result of combining the most unexpected and outlandish decorative elements for a dramatic and eccentric effect.

Into the 'minimal disturbance' bracket might be put ideas such as hanging a huge tapestry made for a much larger formal interior in a small cottage living room, so that it covers an entire wall. It may not have been designed for examination at such close quarters (though this is how the weavers would have seen it), but the craftsmanship that has gone into it can be more easily appreciated this way than if it were hung high on the wall of the hall around the staircase. Large pictures can look very striking in small rooms too, although conversation pieces and landscapes are probably more congenial at close quarters than acres of mythical flesh.

As grand things can feel at ease in small living rooms, so can humble things made for less important rooms or for other countries or even for the garden. Chipped and scruffy, they have found their way into the 'best room' in the house, where they mix happily with their neighbours. An old glass-fronted cupboard of sturdy design which might have hung on a cloakroom wall now sits on the floor with piles of books on top of it, as if it were a table. Old cane garden chairs look quite at home too, and can be dressed up with comfortable, even opulent, cushions. The idea is carried into the display of ornaments: draughtboards hung as pictures, worn garden tools arranged on a shelf, and a series of flower vases from the same pottery in similar milky colours ranged along a mantelpiece as if they were in a manufacturer's showroom. Sometimes a happy overall unity emerges where disparate objects and ornaments all share similar colour tones, and the unconventional *mise en scène*

LEFT AND BELOW In a jumble of bits and pieces the eye picks up the linking elements of a display: the chipped gilding of the picture frame and the flaked plaster of the wall, or the blues and whites of a pile of towels and a cover thrown over an amchair. In the same way a worn white suitcase – an odd intruder in a living room – fits in with the distressed colours of the walls and the different whites in the folds of the chair's upholstery, making it an harmonious corner.

as with a set of received notions evolved over the last hundred years of how things might have been in a cottage. It is arguable whether the careful speculation of prewar arbiters of taste, for example, with their quaint suggestions for cottage decor is any closer to the original cottage reality than the new country look which presents a sort of joyful domestic anarchy.

Some of the most playful and disconcerting interiors today put the gauziest of textiles next to the roughest of stone walls, mix shiny with dull, ancient with modern, grand urban with simple rural. The confidence to create ever more striking and individual combinations without compromising the dignity of an old building or destroying the tranquillity of a new one requires a particular sensitivity to the character of the house, which is why this approach only works where the ideas are a natural expression of an owner's personality and interests, or where collections of objects or pictures have been brought together gradually and with curiosity and love. Collections of local pottery, for example, books, pictures and maps describing the surrounding area give a sense of belonging and make the room a pleasure for visitors, hinting at expeditions that could be made from this comfortable base. Regional furniture connects visually as well as historically with the setting and architecture, being made of the same wood as any panelling or floorboards and for rooms of similar proportions, and local textiles made up as rugs or curtains almost seem made for the room.

FAR LEFT Exciting angles and bright fresh yellow and blue on the walls make a room that looks like a giant child's toy. The timber roof structure and just enough architectural detail saves this new country interior from plainness, while light, blond wood and an ethereal painting remind us of the great outdoors, of big skies above a landscape stretching into the distance and the freedom of unrestricted space.

'*Somewhere between displaying a toboggan – a hint of the setting of the house – and arranging three watering cans on an elegant mantelpiece, a line has been crossed between informality and quirkiness.*'

RIGHT *A purposefully blank green wall and uncurtained windows are matched by straw-coloured flooring so that the room appears almost empty even though it is furnished. Things have been laid out here as if they are on temporary display or might be changed around – like scenery on a set. A picture is propped up on the mantelpiece rather than hung above it and although there is no obvious restraint in the choice of furniture and objects, the overall effect is of clean, sharp outlines and an intentional arrangement. An asymmetrical and eccentric display of old-fashioned metal watering cans also appears contradictorily casual and careful.*

RIGHT *Exotic objects decorate the heavy architecture of a fireplace in a spare decorative scheme which juxtaposes nineteenth-century furniture with ethnic furniture and rugs.*

FAR RIGHT *Evening light infuses this room with the atmosphere and colours of the oil painting, which makes the sea scene appear like a painting within a painting. The pumpkin half-visible in the fireplace and the pots, jugs and bottles arranged above are like two still-life paintings.*

BELOW *A fireplace painted in the blue that has been used for the door frame and dado rail provides a platform for a trundling elephant and a sparkling candelabra.*

*R*ugs complete the room by providing warmth – underfoot and in their colours. Layered they are cosier still. As individual objects, however, they can be used to mark out areas within bigger rooms very effectively. One end of a living room might be 'marked out' as a study or library, the other with a sociable circle of chairs and sofas around a fire. When rugs are laid well, with the best underfelting system, they allow you to appreciate the beauty of the floorboards, parquet or flagstones around them whilst enjoying their warmth and pattern.

Curtains, like rugs, provide punctuation in a room. Weight and feel can be more important than pattern; worn velvet in rusty colours, linen union or thick wool contrast boldly with the rest of the decor or complement it discreetly. Recent pelmet designs have become very elaborate and, perhaps as a reaction, curtain poles have become more popular for country homes, but pelmets are more practical for blocking out the light, and designs for the simplest pelmet shapes which were used in English country house decoration up until the 1960s can provide straightforward yet elegant solutions.

Comfort is crucial to the success of every country living room, and even an austere decorative scheme can be comfortable – though perhaps only to its owner. Of course, comfort means different things in different countries. In the villas of the Bosphorus, lounging sofas around a coffee table in a purpose-made alcove with windows overlooking the sea are essential for entertaining friends at protracted parties of conversation, coffee and sweetmeats. The concept of 'lounging' is central

'Space creates a restfulness not only for the mind, but also for the eye, so that any object can shine in splendid isolation.'

RIGHT *A living room which combines conventional furniture and ornament in an adapted space has picturesque appeal. Roof timbers dip and dive as if they were supporting a complicated fabric tent. A bare terracotta floor, solid stair, simple window seat and ledges here and there make this an informal and engaging interior.*

FAR RIGHT *A warm wood barn interior which is cosy and modern, with lots of traditional features and furniture. It also includes less conventional elements like a wooden toboggan, which is a clue both to the setting of the house and to the outdoor life enjoyed here.*

*F*rom the huge organic shapes of Mediterranean farmhouse fireplaces to the simplest bolection moulding around an English hearth, the architecture of the fireplace is an integral part of the room's decorative scheme. In small cottages it often takes up the whole of an end wall and is the dominant feature of the building and the inglenook fireplace with its built-in seating has a special place in people's hearts. A chimney breast of stone boulder construction is like a primitive stepped sculpture climbing ponderously to the rafters, and has the aspect of an archaeological monument expressing the continuity of life in the house and linking the interior with the landscape setting. It can be the only focus for the room and everything else defers to it.

Besides this rugged creature there are an infinite variety of fireplace styles, shapes and surrounds. Local building tradition and climatic conditions influence them and those that are original to a building are generally the most satisfying, both aesthetically and practically. Fireplace design is probably the least satisfactory feature to 'borrow' from another region for precisely this reason. The most adaptable part of the fireplace, where the opening is simple and relatively small, is its decorative surround. It is sometimes linked with other architectural features in the room, door and window frames, shelving and possibly dado rails, by painting them all the same colour. This imposes a gentle discipline on the room by dividing up its wall spaces and from this the rest of the decoration follows easily.

The country living room of the 1990s reflects the ever-widening range of people's travels and the mixture of influences on tastes. While some feel the greater need to defer to local traditions, others seem to cut themselves loose entirely and trust their own individuality. Never before has there been so much source material available: from books and paintings to the increasing number of historic houses open to the public, as well as films where sophisticated teams of location researchers and set designers create ever more inspirational interiors.

Perfect
KITCHENS & DINING ROOMS

*H*OWEVER MUCH IDEAS CHANGE IN THE DESIGN OF A COUNTRY KITCHEN, ITS AIMS REMAIN THE SAME: TO CREATE A WARM, WELCOMING ATMOSPHERE FOR FRIENDS AND FAMILY, AND TO BE A CONGENIAL AND PRACTICAL PLACE FOR COOKING AND STORING FOOD, POTS AND PANS AND CROCKERY. TODAY, A REACTION AGAINST THE CLUTTERED AND OVER-EQUIPPED KITCHEN OF PAST YEARS IS PROMPTING THE CREATION OF AIRY, SPACIOUS COOKING AND DINING AREAS WHICH ACHIEVE A SIMPLE ELEGANCE WITH THE MINIMUM OF FUSS.

LEFT
*A balance has been struck in a kitchen built
into a larger room. It is practical and
spacious but its low-key design defers to the
elegance of the fireplace and furniture.*

'As cooking becomes simpler – depending on fewer high quality ingredients – so kitchens are becoming correspondingly less elaborate.'

A kitchen reflects the priorities of its cook and all cooks are individuals, but trends do emerge and it seems no accident that as cooking becomes simpler, depending more on fewer high-quality ingredients, so kitchens are becoming correspondingly less elaborate. The country kitchen too now depends on fewer, better-quality utensils, solid furniture and good joinery. That can mean old or new, and it can mean quietly expensive or quietly modest.

Retreating from the extremes of the two major themes in kitchen decor in the last twenty-five years – the crowded displays of bric-a-brac and dried herbs which was the country kitchen and the clinical lines of the approach which borrowed its aesthetic from industrial kitchens – there are middle ways, traditional and quirky ways of arranging a kitchen. Some of these alternative visions have probably been around all along, especially in the unmodernized kitchens of old houses. In them the focus is quite different. The eye is not forced to notice the sleekness of the fitted units to the exclusion of everything else, nor is the spectator so bowled over by the sheer profusion of the china on a dresser or expensive saucepans on the shelves that the possibility of enjoying the individual character of any single piece is removed.

Restraint rather than minimalism is the key and the result is sometimes a kitchen which, unintentionally, begins to look more like its historic antecedents and, more appropriately, complementary to the simple architecture of an old cottage or farmhouse (although there are very few who could forego all the appliances which make modern cooking less of a chore than it was when the house was built).

LEFT *Blackened griddle pans hang on the wall – part-decoration, part-storage solution, and a modern variation on the more traditional display of shiny copper pans. The display of more mundane utensils signals a new enjoyment of their design and materials. Roughly boxed-in plumbing and patchy plaster walls are a picturesque backdrop to the carefully chosen heavy checked curtains.*

RIGHT *This spare modern dining room illustrates a sophisticated version of simplicity where structural features are central to the character of the interior. The lofty space allows full appreciation of the colours and textures of the timber roof and floor, which are separated by the disciplined lines of dark blue painted joinery in a fitted sideboard and pairs of internal and external glass doors around three sides of the room.*

*I*t is surprising how difficult it is to break away from the recent conventions of the fitted kitchen which, as a convenient design solution, has penetrated almost every kitchen in western Europe, America and Australia and many other parts of the globe as well. As a simple idea it works well enough, but the repetition of banal design in the mass-produced units ranged along three walls of a kitchen can have a similarly desecrating effect on an interesting room as slapping a jazzy but inappropriate shop front onto a beautiful building. A fitted kitchen can be cheap and cheerful (though it can also be extremely expensive) and in a tiny kitchen particularly it is often the best solution; but there are other ways of doing it.

It sometimes seems as if mass-produced units force a kitchen into submission rather than letting it have its say. In Mediterranean countries, where there is a ceramic tile manufacturing tradition, country kitchens often have tile-covered counters with open spaces for pans underneath. They are practical, hygienic and architectural in character, so they complement a room rather than looking as if they have been applied to it like make-up. The sharper edges and corners and chunkier proportions make them look like the kitchens of professional cooks, or at least cooks who mean business, rather than those kitchens which look as if they cannot decide whether to be purely decorative or purely functional.

Most of all, these counter-tops have different proportions to the standard fitted unit, 60cm (24in) deep, and one of the most refreshing and successful approaches

FAR LEFT *One gas ring perched on a long wooden chest is enough of a kitchen in this woodland cabin, where simple meals can be prepared without any fuss.*

LEFT *Side by side the old range and a new cooker fit neatly under the broad mantelpiece of an unusual centrally placed chimney, combining the best of the old with the best of the new. In a large open room which serves as kitchen, dining room and living room, this layout is an ideal informal arrangement.*

ABOVE *A generous-sized old-fashioned electric cooker and an unselfconscious and attractive assortment of cooking equipment of different vintages together reflect the priorities of a cook who uses the best tool for the job – regardless of its pedigree.*

LEFT AND RIGHT *The height of this room and the length of its windows give an otherwise average-sized kitchen panache. A disciplined approach to storage and display makes full use of the space: an iron pot stand reaches to the ceiling and shows off the subtle splendours of a collection of toffee-coloured casseroles, terrines and moulds, and between the windows three pot-bellied meat covers have been mounted on the wall.*

to decorating the kitchen is to introduce different proportions in these details – not just for their own sake, but where it would make a kitchen work better. Where the tyranny of the standard depth of worktops and kitchen appliances has been cast off, the effect is startlingly different and liberating.

The kitchen furniture designed between the 1920s and the 1950s, when manufacturers were working slowly towards the fitted kitchen but had not quite got there, is beginning to surface again as an alternative to more recent solutions. A 1950s dresser with its let-down worktop, in pert bright green, seems almost quaint in its modest pretensions to 'convenience', compared to the acres of bogus marble on offer today in every kitchen warehouse. Its clean lines and slim storage capacity are characteristic of a period when cookery and cooking equipment was simpler, in the years before it became an expensive mainstream leisure activity with constantly changing fashions. The large scrubbed-pine kitchen tables of sturdy design around which a large family can eat comfortably have long been popular, but there are also the same tables in miniature which would have stood against the wall or beside the cooker. Wooden vegetable racks with little printed labels to indicate their contents and straightforward shelves on straightforward brackets are old-fashioned and using them would be merely nostalgic if they were not so obviously practical even today.

We have become very used to the idea that long runs of worktops are the priority in a kitchen and of course they are important, but it means that storage – however extensive – is often limited to shallow, high cabinets or squat, deeper cupboards under the worktop. Much more practical and generous is a good, deep floor-to-ceiling cupboard with double doors which can fit things in in different combinations – huge carving plates and tea things, piles of plates and pie dishes. Like the butler's pantry of a hundred years ago, green baize is used to line the shelves where silver is stored, and the glasses can be lined up in regimented rows of graduating size to satisfy the most orderly mind.

house as a fire precaution, so a scheme that throws out a new extension might even find some historical justification. Combining a top-lit design with traditional-sized windows to match the rest of the house can give a refreshing impression of spaciousness without compromising the exterior, and represents a modern departure in so far as the service block has become a presentable part of the house.

Establishing a new space and airiness in a kitchen connects it psychologically to its country setting, but it also focuses attention on the fewer things in the kitchen. Suddenly you can see and appreciate the great flagstone slabs on the floor – which might be the same as those used outside the back door – or the width and pattern of the floorboards in an old house. Building materials are constant echoes of a sense of place, connections which are reinforced, of course, by traditional regional design. The style of a Tuscan kitchen fireplace, for example, built upon a platform about 45cm (18in) from the ground is quite different from the wider, lower fireplace in an English farmhouse. The latter usually has a stove installed in the opening nowadays, whereas in Italy the fireplace is still used for a good blaze or perhaps some cooking *alla brace*. Logs are stacked up in an arched recess underneath, ready to stoke the fire.

Unchanging rural tradition has a lot to teach too about good honest design, in everything from pots and pans to bread ovens and smoking chambers, cool larders and flooring materials. The simplest things – like a wooden roller-towel hanger on the back of a door, the carefully gouged channels of a wooden draining board, the colours of slate shelving in a pantry or the texture of green baize in a cutlery drawer – catch the eye because of the care that has gone into their manufacture and because of their obvious practicality.

FAR LEFT *The glazes of dark brown and black ceramics catch the light, while the outlines of a wooden barrel and ironware emerge as dull shapes creating strange chiaroscuro effects in this kitchen storeroom. Anything which does not blend with its limited colour range is excluded.*

LEFT *An old Australian dresser has a simple, functional design and clean, unfussy lines. The locks and plain panelled doors give it the look of a kitchen safe. In contrast to the open shelves of Welsh and English dressers, everything is shut away, and instead of yellowy pine it is made of richly coloured native timbers.*

ABOVE *Humble kitchen utensils make a wonderful display even in everyday use. Graduated sizes of wooden chopping boards are patterned with the crosshatching of years of use, while different shapes of sieves and metal saucepan lids catch the light across their uneven surfaces.*

*T*he difference today is that people are choosing simplicity, and the individuality of their approach results in the creation of new combinations of old and new and quirky juxtapositions that suit their particular lifestyles. Kitchens are peppered with discreet little contrasts of simplicity and sophistication. In a one-room wooden cabin, you would expect to see a kettle and a couple of plates, but not necessarily the pair of Georgian rummers or the packet of good coffee beans. Apart from this, there is little room for paraphernalia – the campbed is only a step away and a typewriter takes up most of the table space. The confidence to get rid of unnecessary things and to concentrate on those utensils and pieces of furniture that are important to you for their sentimental, historic or practical value, is a driving force in these rough but comfortable country interiors.

Comfortable, but not so rough, are the kitchens designed on a more generous scale, modern but appreciative of old things where they make sense. The starting point is a lofty room where cooking and eating are done in the same space. The aim is to keep everything quite plain and functional but to make sure that in its details and materials it uses the best quality for the job. The fittings are unfussy, the shelves

OPPOSITE PAGE *In the kitchen of a railway carriage a stand has been taken against the seamless monotony of fitted units. Salvaged enamelware buckets, kettles and baby churns decorate the shelves; even the cream and green paintwork takes its cue from a frying pan and colander.*

LEFT *Bright red pot stands provide the perfect counterpoint for rich green walls and painted furniture. One carefully chosen object can influence a whole interior.*

ABOVE *In contrast to a bright ethnic scheme, drab greens and browns point up the asceticism of this log cabin kitchen.*

"Individuality of approach results in quirky juxtapositions and original combinations of old and new that suit particular styles of life."

RIGHT *A spacious but low-ceilinged farmhouse kitchen owes its distinctive character to the unfashionable glossy brown of its painted ceiling, which nevertheless reflects the warm colours of the fire. The same colour is used on the huge fireplace surround, the dado and a cooker hood in the corner. It is countered by an old-fashioned buttery yellow above dado level. Most modern kitchens are so emphatically bright that this atmospheric solution seems instantly appealing simply because it is different. Colour schemes need to be constantly reinvented both to find fresh ideas and to escape from the powerful influence of fashion.*

LEFT *Views through a door and an internal window in this neutral interior reveal a light-filled dining room where grey-green paint has been used to tie the architectural details together in a taut, spare decorative scheme. The furnishing of this house is not a result of the casual accumulation of bits and pieces but rather a careful filtering out of any distracting objects from a clear, focused vision. The poised restraint becomes a backdrop for blazes of colour in the temporary but abundant displays of glass and china on a sideboard or flowers on a table.*

RIGHT *With all the quiet browns, greys and whites of this interior, a disciplined two-colour arrangement of flowers might have been expected to complement it, but perhaps it is a mark of respect and a recognition of the vibrance of natural colours that this jug full of bright blooms should be allowed to bring the room to life so completely. The flowers seem to be teasing their surroundings for being so subdued. Contrasting with a roughly made trestle table and benches, a fragile lace curtain falls to the floor at the window, adding a feminine element to this robust room.*

'The new spareness is about restraint rather than minimalism, but it also embraces a lightness of touch and a sense of humour.'

of metal plumbing pipes which, a few years ago, would have been hidden away in elaborate boxes of clever joinery, are allowed to run purposefully towards their destinations in full view. Where plastic pipes are to be installed in a new kitchen, in contrast, they would be carefully boxed in. Pride is taken in the solid old plumbing with its wall brackets and chunky joints, whereas today's casual assembly of plastic tubes is not thought well designed enough to be on show.

Unfussy fittings that promise years of use, an absence of gimmicks and fashionable decorative touches, good materials and solid workmanship characterize the country kitchen today. Where old or old-fashioned elements are used, it is because they work, not because they lend picturesqueness to the room.

Perfect
BEDROOMS & BATHROOMS

*W*HATEVER THE PLAY ON EXPECTATIONS IN A BEDROOM'S DECORATION, THE MOST IMPORTANT THING IS THAT YOU CAN SLEEP WELL IN IT. OF ALL THE ROOMS IN THE HOUSE THE BEDROOMS SHOULD BE THE MOST TRANQUIL AND RESTFUL IN ARRANGEMENT, COLOUR SCHEME AND MATERIALS. THERE CAN BE SURPRISES TOO, BUT OF A GENTLE KIND: A TWIST HERE AND THERE IN A CONVENTIONAL DECORATIVE SCHEME GIVES A BEDROOM FRESHNESS, BUT NOTHING TOO BOISTEROUS THAT MIGHT THREATEN A PEACEFUL NIGHT'S SLEEP.

LEFT AND ABOVE
In a bedroom refreshingly stripped of soft furnishings, silver brushes and photographs crowd a table – reminders of family, friends and, like the model boat above, of childhood.

*T*he classic country bedroom of recent times is instantly recognizable today as a series of pretty clichés: a four-poster bed, a quilt, a colour scheme of whites and pale pinks, yellows, or blues, and mounds of lacy cushions. This pastel fantasy is in danger of becoming a little cloying and a breath of fresh air has, in response, begun to blow through the country bedroom.

Small changes can make all the difference, but perhaps the biggest change is a switch of focus away from too many rich soft furnishings – floor-length bedside table covers, thickly interlined curtains and elaborate pelmets – towards the spatial character of the room and its architectural features. And just as fewer soft furnishings bring out the room's essential character, so fewer pieces of interesting furniture complement it.

The traditional bedrooms of Mediterranean farmhouses perfectly illustrate the call to spaciousness, with proportions which sometimes seem to be borrowed from an opera set. In a farmhouse bedroom in Spain or Italy an antique bed of generous size, with a wrought iron or wooden bedhead, sheets of coarse linen and rough blankets in drab colours, rests in splendid isolation in uncompromising acres of beautifully craggy terracotta floor. There are no unnecessary props, no matching bedside lights nor bedside rugs the size of postage stamps, no lacy cushions nor baskets of magazines. A cupboard of impressive size with double doors and bold carving or painted decoration stands against a wall; there might be chairs and a table used as a desk, but little more. The walls are rough textured and light floods in through a tall window. The loftiness of the room is emphasized by the exposed workings of the roof, and the browns and pinks of its timbers and tiles mirror the floor below.

Whether the room is in the most rugged farmhouse, where the walls are whitewashed stone and the door opens directly onto the farmyard, or in a more genteel country home, the furniture does not need to match the social standing of

"Bedroom furniture which promises comfort in a rudimentary setting is like a civilized encampment, and a surreal juxtaposition is created as the setting becomes simpler and the bed more elegant."

RIGHT *This dramatic bedroom could be in a palace or a garden building, but instead of playing up to either of these notions it follows an individual course in an exuberant, personal style. An eccentric mix of furniture is combined with jugs of wild flowers in a vast, undecorated space and highlighted with splashes of acid colour.*

FAR RIGHT *Traditional elements of simple country furnishing have been chosen for a converted railway carriage. Lace curtains and a wrought iron bedstead are arranged alongside a trunk used as a bedside table in a wagon lit bedroom.*

but not matched. An iron bedstead, the lack of ornament and the blankness of the single colour recall at first a 1920s sanatorium – all hygiene and functionalism, light and airiness. But the introduction of the gaily coloured elements retrieves the room from any atmosphere of austerity or bleakness that might accompany these associations and creates something new, serene and comfortable.

Large airy bedrooms are not always easy to create, but spaciousness is often achieved in a smaller house with careful planning and perhaps the sacrifice of a room or a rearrangement of rooms. Compromise and a certain amount of lateral thinking may turn up the perfect solution and the help of an architect can be invaluable to suggest options that may not have been raised before. By making spaciousness a priority in the early stages of decoration, rather than having fixed ideas, much can be achieved in a smaller house.

Many people, though, are able to make perfect bedrooms, complete with all comforts, in smaller attic spaces. In the traditional one-and-a-half-storey cottage found all over northern Europe these spaces were built to be used as bedrooms.

*R*ather than disguise the rough-hewn timbers, or even a reinforced steel joist, rather than paper the sloping ceilings and fill in the angles of the roof space with cupboards, the country bedroom is left with its rough edges. Into this setting, in complete contrast, the most generous and comfortable bed is introduced. A large bed in a small room may take up most of the space, but it makes the room into an inviting nest. Rammed up against the wall with room only for a night table and some books this bedroom is an eyrie, where you can lie in bed and feel safe and listen to the wind chasing round the chimney or enjoy the view from the window. The best country beds are high enough to climb into; they stand well off the ground to avoid draughts, but they also have deep mattresses which make them higher still. Good linen, generous pillows and perhaps a bolster or a paisley-patterned eiderdown are unchanging elements in the perfect bedroom. It does not matter if any or all of these elements are old and scruffy; in fact, a worn and faded look is often gentler and more comfortable than the sharpness of the brand new.

Bedroom furniture which promises comfort in an otherwise rudimentary setting is like a very civilized encampment. As the setting becomes simpler and the bed more elegantly arranged within it a surreal juxtaposition is created, and at the extremes of this stylistic tendency are some truly eccentric bedrooms where boldness and striking

FAR LEFT *A highly varnished cupboard bed is reminiscent of the compact design of the interior of a classic yacht, bringing a hint of glamour to a rural idea.*

LEFT *Where regional furniture is used locally, architecture and interior enjoy the closest relationship. Here the furnishings fit the room in their proportions and designs, and the graining and colour of the wood matches those of the walls, floor and door. Details like the simple metal door handle also follow regional designs.*

ABOVE *Framed like a picture and with a curious shutter-like door to close it away, this Dutch cupboard bed is made of broad upright planks like those used for the floor.*

'A bedroom with a small roof span is like a perfect wooden tent.'

ABOVE *Lit by dormer windows and defined by the strong lines and patterns created by its wooden roof, this sparely furnished attic bedroom is still comfortable.*

RIGHT *The rough timbers of an Italian farmhouse are civilized by warm rugs and elegant furniture. Even though the room is not enormous, everything about it is of generous proportions, from the expanse of window to the size of the bed and the length of the stool at its foot.*

OPPOSITE PAGE *A wooden tent of a roof and the barest wooden bedstead make for indoor camping with a view.*

*T*he cupboard bed's open-air cousin is the cot bed. It can be the simplest box on legs – built against a wall or freestanding – and would have been filled with a rough mattress and covered with coarse blankets. It was probably the most common sort of bed in cottage homes, and would have been knocked up on the spot. A more genteel version, with carved posts and ends and tapered legs, is to be found in Scandinavian homes and is often used as a day bed. Worn staining on its pine planks gives it an air of informal scruffiness which a proud householder of generations ago would surely not have put up with. Today this gentle fading is appreciated both for its pattern and as evidence that the bed has enjoyed and continues to enjoy a long and useful life.

Memories and associations make old things precious and a bedroom full of treasured furniture, books and pictures becomes a three-dimensional family album. It might include a grandmother's dressing-table set laid out as it used to be for an elaborate toilette, photographs of friends and relatives, favourite things from childhood and perhaps some well-thumbed books. The history of each object is like a piece of a jigsaw which, once put together, gives the room its special character.

RIGHT *The unselfconscious summer-camp feel of this dark wood attic bedroom is enhanced by simple furnishings. An old-fashioned unlined textured material is used for the curtains, in keeping with the atmosphere of a warm wooden cabin, and the bold red is echoed in the canvas camp-bed, striped mattress cover and woven floor rug laid on bare, unpolished floorboards.*

LEFT *A cheerful mixture of patterns and colours on an unpainted day bed fits with the strong blues and reds of the room. The uneven surface of the log wall and its deep, dark lines are structural characteristics which also work as decorative features.*

ABOVE *The teddy bears seem unconcerned by their eccentric home in a house built into rocks. The scene recalls children's picture books where bedrooms are transported lock, stock and barrel to faraway places.*

*T*wo- or three-colour theming works much better, but again only if it is done in a relaxed way. It is perhaps most successful where the individual elements in a room do not at first seem to fit together and appear to have nothing in common in terms of style, material, provenance or history except a shared colour range. In this situation the colours unify the room, and impose a gentle order and calm which is particularly reassuring in a bedroom.

With the return to a humbler country ideal, the Edwardians chose to dedicate rooms to particular country flowers. The architect Baillie Scott who, like many of his generation, also designed gardens, felt the importance of retaining garden themes in the decoration and he talks about using real flowers in his schemes for decoration as well as designing them into bed covers and cushions – 'not executed in the hurried modern way but done gradually as funds and time allow'.

To provide a fitting backdrop for flowers, Baillie Scott also suggested that a bedroom should be finished without pattern and adornments. This idea has returned and more and more country bedrooms are washed with unusual neutral colours like lilacs, greys, the lightest browns and greens. These bedrooms are serene as they stand, with wooden furniture, white linen, airiness and space, but they are brought to life by flowers; not in fabrics, or wallpapers, or in painted decoration, but spilling out of jugs and vases. Waking up in a comfortable bed to the smell of narcissi, hyacinths or lilies you could be forgiven for thinking that nothing else was needed to make a country bedroom perfect.

*I*n houses with porches and outer hallways the threshold is an unclear line, underlining the close relationship of the house with its setting. Flagstones used in a porch or up the garden path continue into the hall of the house, and logs are stored to dry just outside the door and brought in to another resting post in a log basket before being carried to the fire.

Logs for the fire, keys for the door, letters waiting to be posted, torches for the dark trek at night to close up the greenhouse, fishing rods and other sports gear are all found in the hall in picturesque chaos or in careful order. The hall is a busy place with doors leading off it, perhaps a passage through to the back of the house or the staircase – a defining element of its function as a point of departure.

A hall often provides a viewpoint for looking into other rooms, or even through one room into another whose light and colours, furniture and fireplace are framed in the doorway. It needs to have a strong enough decorative scheme to balance what can be glimpsed beyond, but its character must not be too overbearing or the other rooms lose their interest and power to encourage exploration.

'A hall provides a viewpoint for looking into other rooms, whose light and colours, furniture and fireplace are framed in the doorway.'

LEFT *A mixture of traditional hall features and modern ideas are brought together to create an interior of contrasts. An unusual version of tongue-and-groove panelling made of thick and thin planking provides a minimal design for the walls and instead of more conventional door surrounds a discreet groove moulding outlines the doorway. There are no skirting boards here but they reappear in the room beyond and wide floorboards painted battleship grey in both rooms provide a unifying link. A simple but elegant country hall bench sits below a contrastingly sophisticated mirror, framed with elaborate cornucopias and surmounted by an eagle.*

RIGHT *A corner of a hall has been turned into a study by the simple expedient of close-hanging a group of prints to define a wall area and placing a desk and chair below it. Box files and a tub of pens share the space with a miniature obelisk, and they all fit in with the subtle browns and greys of the room's colouring. Limiting the colour range of the chaos on most desks might seem a challenge but here it has worked.*

'The hall is an introduction not only to the house but also to the personality of its owner, whose interests are reflected here.'

simple wooden designs. Wooden staircases today might be left bare, or alternatively they might have just their risers painted to match balusters or walls, or they might be painted all over. Bare staircases are popular, but life is quieter in a small house if a stair carpet is fitted down its centre and attached, perhaps with stair rods. If carpeting is being chosen purely for practicality, with other floors being left bare except for occasional rugs, dark rough-woven stair carpet can be laid so that it does not become a distracting feature. Stone staircases, though they may seem cold, often look best when they are left completely bare.

The stairwell itself provides the biggest stretch of uninterrupted wall space in the house and is ideal for hanging a tapestry or pictures so that the hall becomes a gallery. Treated like this the hall is an introduction not only to the house but also to the personality of its owner, whose interests are reflected here.

screens covered in tooled leather or dark heavy velvet are sometimes used to perform the same function. Another traditional way of solving the draught problem is to hang very heavy wool (like loden) as a curtain on a pole across the front door, as is done in the country churches of Germany and Austria. Fumbling through the thick folds of a rough drab-coloured curtain for the door handle, you really feel that you are leaving the warmth for the chill outside.

Unusual neutral colours work very well in halls and dividing the walls up with a painted or actual dado, which runs up the stairs, can help to define and bring order to what can be a rather muddled architectural space in a little country cottage. A neutral colour which echoes, in slightly lighter shades, the honey colours of a stone floor, or complements the wooden staircase and door frames, enables splashes of colour to be used in picture mounts, rugs or flowers on a hall table. Some subdued but stronger colours like buffs, creamy browns and chalky maroons recall the colours of the back-passage areas of grander country houses, and although these were originally chosen for their practicality in not showing the dirt, they can also be good colours against which to hang pictures. The lighter neutral colours create a slightly more elegant atmosphere while strong reds, greens and blues look more exotic. Colour schemes often have strong associations even while they succeed in creating something new and different, and inspiration for them can come from anywhere, from a piece of material, from a glimpse into the hallway of a house seen from the street, from the endpapers of a book, or from pictures. Combinations of two or three colours which in the abstract appear unsuited to each other suddenly seem to work when spotted together in an unlikely setting.

'An atmosphere of mystery is created in a sparely furnished hall where attention focuses on its essential character.'

FAR LEFT *A staircase landing becomes a study where a large table fits neatly into the space between rooms. The undecorated space is a striking contrast to the crowded desk.*

LEFT *Lit on two sides, a cubby hole overlooks the garden and makes a little studio protected from the weather.*

RIGHT *Painted furniture plays an important part in this interior, where a chair is painted the same colour as the wall against which it stands, and the soft green of a wooden desk is continued in the bedroom furniture beyond. Its atmosphere is calm and light, rather than oppressively planned.*

LEFT *A cheerfully uncontrived jumble of paraphernalia shows the hall as a picturesque and ever-changing dumping ground. High ceilings, a proper old butler's table, and a bell system linked to all the rooms of the house are typical of an English country house. The back quarters of these houses, once the exclusive preserve of servants, possessed their own elegance which stems from their spaciousness, simple decoration, and solid fixtures and fittings.*

RIGHT *A quirky interpretation of conventional hall arrangements becomes an eccentric still life using disparate elements. Mimicking a grand console table, a wooden slatted table-top has been placed on two carved wooden legs in front of an elegant dado. A box of tools, a silver teapot and some framed lace take up most of the space.*

A scheme that plays safe with lighter neutral colours and leaves bolder colour to the furnishings is less likely to date quickly than a bright and exciting new combination, but there is a difference between playing safe and going for the lowest common denominator, which produces a bland characterless interior. A scheme of quiet colours needs to be chosen as carefully as the loudest design.

Introducing a vibrant colour scheme into an otherwise conventional hall arrangement jolts it out of complacency. Conversely, when a conventional backdrop plays host to a witty arrangement of furniture and objects the results are successful too. It is a difficult game to play because anything too planned can look self-conscious or plain foolish, but there is no substitute for a sure eye and a genuine interest in the architecture, furniture and ornaments being juggled with.

The saddest thing you can do to a hall is not to use its front door. Many people unthinkingly get into the habit of using a back door, and gradually the front door loses its point and the hall becomes a useless passage which shows signs of being unloved and seems to miss the bustle of activity. Abandoning the front door affects the external elevation and garden planting schemes no longer highlight its importance as the front entrance. The house's orientation changes and with it something is lost, unless the change is carefully planned and thought out within the overall decoration and arrangement of the house.

ABOVE *The honey-coloured stone of this Italian hall provides a dappled backdrop for the few pieces of furniture and pictures and its uneven surface animates the interior. A carved date panel above the door, stair tread mouldings and a niche punctuate the walls and underline the importance of stone. Soft grey walls provide a neutral foil, and red mounts to two groups of architectural prints put the final touch to the whole.*

LEFT *The rich subtle colouring of garden fruits brings to life any little corner where they lie. Here a pitted stone garden basin has a good flat surround upon which to put apples and plums before rinsing. A task usually carried out in a less picturesque kitchen sink becomes a pleasurable experience in the open air.*

RIGHT *This outdoor room combines the advantages of the height of a balcony with the space of a terrace. A simple lean-to shelter has been built against the main house and its pink pantiles dotted with lichens are like a camouflage in this landscape. The roof rests on sturdy timbers and provides some protection from the elements so there is space for eating outside in full sun or shade. A broad, plain parapet extends the seating area although climbing roses are beginning to invade it. From the comfort of this luxurious spot there are wide views of surrounding farmland and hills.*

Formality and informality in gardens and in the layout of the buildings immediately around a house in the country have always taken turns to be in fashion. Combined in different measures, they have been the most distinctive themes of garden history all over the world. In the development of every style, an element of informality in a formal garden, or vice versa, expresses something slightly different. Informality might be championed as an expression of respect for 'nature', or as enthusiastic acceptance of its wildness, or out of romantic impulse. Formality on the other hand might be the result of careful husbandry, a love of balance and symmetry, or simply a restraining hand. Managed unruliness and elegant formality both require intensive labour but of a kind so good for the soul that, for many, gardening is the only therapy to counteract an otherwise stressful life.

Embracing nature without having to put in the hours of toil also has its supporters in a laissez-faire approach which would be anathema to anyone with gardening ambitions. It involves dismissing completely the idea of planting protective garden hedges, or building brick walls or a picket fence to mark out your private patch of territory and guard your home life from the uncertainties of the big wide world. It

'Everyone draws energy from a garden's tranquillity, and in the design of a garden special vantage points are introduced to provide cues for reflection and enjoyment of its views.'

ABOVE *A private courtyard sheltered by a dramatic cliff with plants tumbling down its bumpy face provides a picturesque outdoor eating area.*

RIGHT *A tree filters sun and breezes on this terrace. The red stone retains the sun's heat well into a summer evening providing comforting, natural 'underfloor' heating.*

FAR RIGHT *Half-indoors, half-outdoors, this terrace is open to the elements on one side and enclosed with a window on the other. Different solutions evolve to cope with the often capricious demands of particular microclimates.*

involves cutting the ties with a tradition of taming the land and working the earth and, instead, it welcomes the wilderness in. The instinctive nurturing of a plot of land is exchanged for a less possessive appreciation of one's surroundings.

This idealism is more appropriate in some places than in others. A house in an isolated woodland clearing or on a sandy dune, or even one on an unspoilt hillside, can be ruined by a garden that has been brutally tacked on, whereas a garden on a village street which shares its boundaries with neighbours also shares a history of cultivation and this should be respected. The uncultivated surroundings of a converted farm building need the most sensitive intervention to prevent them looking suburban, and it is sometimes more striking to leave the tangled grasses and scrubby trees and at most to introduce more indigenous wild grasses and flowers.

When sensitivity to the integrity of the landscape – whether managed or wild – guides the choice of approach, the making of a garden often becomes a project involving research into the history of the area, its plant species, fruit trees and vegetables. It might also include looking at how cultivation has moulded the local landscape and how that character might be reflected in the garden scheme.

BELOW *Most verandahs have a lean-to roof design but this one is like a self-contained cabin open on three sides. It is fully furnished as an outdoor living room with a bench running along the length of the back wall covered in sprigged cotton cushions and pictures on the wall. An openwork balustrade is like a fence between the verandah and the meadow beyond. Deep overhanging eaves give it the character of a garden summer house.*

RIGHT *Verandahs vary in design from country to country. Here a Long Island house has a shingle back wall and no balustrade dividing the furnished platform from the garden. Rocking chairs and swing seats are often of local design and catch every whisper of breeze, and during the hot weather beds may even be moved outdoors.*

*T*he most successful gardens are often those which find a middle way, where nature and the gardener appear to jostle affectionately. The former gives way here to allow some imaginative underplanting of a clump of trees while the gardener sometimes allows picturesque incursions by wild undergrowth at the outposts of a plot. Here boundaries blur so that the garden blends into the wildness beyond, and its vulnerability is underscored by the speed with which nature reclaims territory.

Even this good-natured picture is an illusion, though, because it is the gardener who chooses where to allow the mutiny. It will not be tolerated in the middle of a deep and carefully orchestrated border, nor in the inviolable calm and order of the kitchen garden, where a return to the traditions of careful husbandry has been fuelled by a growing distaste for intensively farmed produce and an appreciation that home-grown vegetables and fruit eaten in their season and fresh from the plot have an unrivalled flavour.

The warm glow of justifiable pride induced by the sight of neat rows of potatoes and onions, lettuces and feathery leaved carrots, beans trained up wigwams of wooden stakes or the tips of asparagus peeping out of the soil on a spring morning is one of the greatest pleasures for a country gardener. Planted out to delight as well as to provide a home-grown harvest, the vegetable garden shows how humble plants can produce a stunning display enclosed in beds edged with workmanlike

wood planks as if they were giant vegetable crates. Paths of gravel or beaten earth, soft pink bricks laid in a herringbone pattern or simple flagstones unify the layout like a sort of horizontal scaffolding.

The threat of having this hard work ruined by birds and rabbits produces a varied and often comically defiant array of home-made devices: nets like webs draped over fruit bushes and dotty cages of wood and wire protect the precious crop, while drunken scarecrows who do not look well-dressed enough to stand guard over the tidy rows glower into the middle distance. The gardener often seems to lose his sense of the garden's dignified elegance when it comes to bird and rabbit deterrents, and a surreal folk-art aspect gives this corner of the garden an unselfconscious jollinesss which can make sophisticated planting schemes elsewhere seem almost humourless by comparison.

Nearby, the gardener's refuge is his potting shed, perhaps a picturesquely ramshackle affair with a rainwater butt and cold frames against it. Stacks of very plain but weathered terracotta pots and worn wooden-handled tools show evidence of years of use. Here, as in the kitchen, some of the newfangled garden gadgets have been weeded out in favour of traditional tools which have lasted longer and have done their job efficiently for generations. They have a quiet aesthetic of their own derived from simple good design and solid materials.

ABOVE *Chunky wooden planking makes a solid deck, and its nautical associations are echoed in the design of the wooden railing and stairway. Instead of deck chairs there is a garden bench and a wooden planter, and instead of sea spray, foliage seeps into every crevice. Open to the elements, the deck is an ideal outdoor room for milder climates and for gardeners who are happier with leisurely pottering than back-breaking toil. It is a peaceful spot looking out into the treetops with just the birds – and a dog here – for company; it is a place for quiet reflection.*

LEFT *A low-ceilinged potting shed-cum-flower room has a gardener's bench running along one side under greenhouse windows. Instead of seed trays and heaps of earth, elegant urns and ceramic jugs crowd its surface. Baskets which might be used for indoor bulbs hang from the roof and tiny flower pots are ranged along the wall, but a cushioned cane chair suggests that this is more than just a functional storeroom.*

RIGHT *More of a greenhouse than a conservatory, this outdoor room has been tacked onto a clapboard house. Unlike many modern conservatories which have highly polished floors and bright white prefabricated frames, this has a gentleness which derives from the colour of its bleached wood frame and furniture and rough floor. A decorative but functional slatted bench, a stack of cane supports and two old watering cans make an unselfconscious display which is part of the appeal of this plant lover's den.*

'*The traditional contents of the potting shed have a quiet aesthetic of their own, derived from simple good design and solid materials.*'

*T*he fastidious order of the vegetable garden is often countered by a scatterbrained mess in the potting shed, showing where the gardener's priorities lie, but the keen handyman has a quite different lair whose toolshed and workbench are paragons of neatness. All the mysterious equipment for a hundred in-hand projects are fixed like displayed butterflies on a wall of brackets and loops and holes and each tool has its allotted place. Graduated families of chisels, spanners, screwdrivers and little drawers of bits and bobs are part of a functional display which illustrates the creativity celebrated here.

The outbuildings around a house in the country provide little vignettes of the talents and skills of the owner of the place, and form an architectural index of the sort of life led here. A clapboard boathouse with a shingle roof, an applestore with its wooden slatted shelves and musty smell, a log store with its scarred wooden horse and beautifully stacked chunks and slivers of winter fuel, all combine to help to define the special character of the place.

Livestock have their own homes which can be picturesque or utilitarian. The architectural history of the dog kennel is as rich as one could wish and full of

LEFT *Although the path from the garden gate to the front door is short and straight the ramshackle fence and informal pergola make it a delightful ramble under climbing, spreading branches with a view of a clear pool of sunshine in front of the house. Garden structures made from weather bleached timbers blend readily into the planting scheme of a garden.*

RIGHT *A hilltop belvedere like a castle rampart commands wide views over the surrounding countryside, which shimmers in the sun. A solid parapet contains a spreading terrace paved with terracotta. Pots of geraniums and overhanging trees enliven its plain lines, while a table and chairs take up the only available shade.*

necessary paraphernalia for working and an odd selection of inspirational talismans: a favourite cup, a particularly comfortable chair and other bits and pieces make their way here. The unselfconscious accumulation, which combines primitive conditions with the odd indispensable luxury from a more sophisticated world, makes an intriguing and engaging scene.

It is not just artists who seek seclusion and inspiration in a garden; everyone draws energy from its tranquillity and in the design of a garden special vantage points are introduced to provide cues for reflection and enjoyment of its views. In the eighteenth century these may have been pavilions – with views up the slopes of Vesuvius to the menacing tip of the volcano and in the other direction out over the Bay of Naples – or they might have been neo-classical temples overlooking English lakes carefully engineered by man rather than God. By the beginning of this century garden vistas were generally designed on a more domestic scale in the compartmentalized gardens still popular today. In a series of 'garden rooms' defined by hedges, belts of trees, or walls, the gardener is able to create different schemes within one garden, with formal and informal plantings along a variety of themes. Vantage points command views along 'walks' or through these garden rooms, providing opportunities for contemplation, conversation and living outdoors.

To furnish these vantage points, garden seats of wood or stone under arches of foliage are more likely to be found nowadays than the cool pavilions of two hundred years ago. A bench at the end of a woodland walk, a clapboard summer house

*T*erraces and courtyards close to a house provide a more contained outdoor room, which can be furnished – with a slight shift in key – as if they were interiors. A sofa is replaced by a swinging seat with a cherry-red canvas canopy and buttoned and piped cushions, which look as if they were designed for a yacht, whilst cane or wood tables and chairs make up the scene. The use of containers for shrubs and annuals makes gardening portable and pots are moved round to furnish these outdoor rooms; they decorate terrace parapets, take centre stage at the end of a vista, or frame a distant view. Pots are changed to suit the seasons and moved from indoors to outdoors to mark the beginning of spring, rekindling the relationship between house and garden after the winter.

The convents and monasteries of southern Italy had the right idea about outdoor rooms. Living an enclosed life, these communities often boasted a closed courtyard garden or cloister, with its central well and formal planting, and terraces or a pergola overlooking a dramatic sweep of countryside or coast. Views down into the deep valleys of the Amalfi coast, for example, are punctuated by the terraces of lemon trees and vines until the eye reaches the craggy shoreline and the blue-green sea. The feeling of distance from the hurly-burly of everyday life is palpable. Some convents had rooftop gardens with a distant view framed in the arch from which hung the convent bell. All these gardens provide the perfect place for cool walks, quiet reflection and prayer – as essential nowadays as they have always been.

FAR LEFT *Few things make a householder prouder than to be able to produce home-grown food on a little plot. The hard work all seems worth it when plump vegetables appear. Bee-keeping requires knowledge and intuition and though hives may seem to the outsider to occupy out-of-the-way positions on the fringes of woodland or garden, it suits the bees perfectly.*

LEFT *Gardeners use some odd-looking devices to encourage their crops: inverted flower pots on stakes and whirligig bean poles make this a jaunty corner.*

ABOVE *Down tools: a hoe and a giant ceramic basin lie abandoned on the path, their earthy colours and shapes making them look quite at home as furnishing for this outdoor room.*

'The perfect outdoor room has far-reaching views of the surrounding landscape and a feeling of distance from the hurly-burly of everyday life which is palpable.'

LEFT *Borrowed from nature, this little patch is really only a tiny bite of the surrounding hillside. It has been domesticated not with careful cultivation but with rigged-up running water, a washing slab and duckboarding. The rickety fence keeps nothing out or in and its charm lies in its picturesque irregularity.*

RIGHT *The outdoor room* par excellence*: a bird house in the treetops has splendid views in every direction and still manages to enjoy some protection from harsher weather conditions. Modern materials have been used and modern architecture has devised the latest design solutions, no doubt informed by the expert opinion of ornithologists. Is this the perfect getaway in which to live in peace and at one with nature?*

*I*n less hospitable terrain a garden has to be wrested from nature, making its shelter and tranquillity even more startling. At Lindisfarne on the northeast coast of England, Gertrude Jekyll created a tiny garden a few hundred yards from the romantic castle remodelled in 1903 by Lutyens for Edward Hudson, the owner of *Country Life* magazine. On scrubby, salty, low-lying pasture she built a beautiful but simple stone-walled enclosure which provided shelter for a formal layout. Instead of being an extension of the house, the garden has become a special diversion, requiring a purposeful trot across the windswept space to discover its enchantment.

An enchanting garden is a precious thing – a self-contained world of its own – and keen gardeners spend their lives straining towards this perfection of atmosphere. Success lies in a complex cocktail of happy chance in its siting and setting, simple and sophisticated taste blended together, knowledge and skill, and an individual inventiveness which brings a fresh twist to conventional ideas. As in the arrangement of the interior of the house, the past provides as much inspiration as is required, but taking things a step further or adjusting them to a modern way of life produces new solutions for the outdoor room. Clean-cut or blowsy, formal or informal, pocket-sized or park-sized, a garden is just borrowed from nature for the twinkling of an eye and its very fragility makes it the most poignant element of the home in the country.

*I*NDEX

ACKNOWLEDGMENTS

Publisher's Acknowledgments

We would like to thank the following photographers and organizations for their permission to reproduce the photographs in this book:

1 Nina Dreyer; 2-3 David George; 4-5 Todd Eberle (Designer: Jeffrey Cayle); 6-7 Hotze Eisma; 7 right Ianthe Ruthven (Designers: Alfred Cochrane Associates); 8 left Peter Aprahamian; 8 right Arcaid/Julie Phipps; 9 Jeff McNamara; 10 Ianthe Ruthven (Designer: Amanda Douglas); 11 Peter Woloszynski/The Interior Archive; 12-13 Ianthe Ruthven (Architect/owners: Nicholas Groves-Raines & Kristin Hannesdottir); 13 right Jean-Pierre Godeaut (Stylist: Catherine Ardouin) / Marie Claire Maison; 14-15 Joe Cornish; 15 right Georgia Glynn-Smith; 16 above left and below right Simon McBride; 16 above right John Miller; 17 Simon McBride; 18 Photograph: Hickey Robertson (Jacomini), from Southern Accent magazine; 20 John Miller; 21 Joe Cornish; 22 John Miller; 23 Richard Waite; 24 Patricia Aithie/Ffotograff; 25 David George; 26-27 S & O Mathews; 27 right Marianne Majerus; 28-29 Solvi Dos Santos; 30 Jessie Walker; 31 Richard Felber; 32 left Solvi Dos Santos; 32-33 Nina Dreyer; 33 right Solvi Dos Santos; 34-35 Fritz von der Schulenburg/The Interior Archive; 35 right Solvi Dos Santos; 36 left Peter Woloszynski/ Elizabeth Whiting & Associates; 36-37 Mads Mogensen; 36 right Nina Dreyer; 38 Todd Eberle; 38-39 Paul Ryan/International Interiors (John Saladino); 40 Tim Beddow/The Interior Archive (Nicky Samuel); 40-41 Simon McBride; 42 left Richard Bryant/Arcaid/(Architect: Michael Wilford) courtesy: STO AG; 42-43 Paul Ryan/ International Interiors (Jo Naham); 44-45 Simon McBride ; 45 right Jean-Pierre Godeaut (Maison Maurice, Alsace); 46-47 John Miller; 47 right Fritz von der Schulenberg/The Interior Archive (The Ulster American Folk Park); 48-49 Simon McBride; 48 left Ianthe Ruthven; 50 Julie Phipps)/Arcaid (Architect: Chris Cowper/Cower Griffith Brimblecombe Associates, Whittlesford, Cambridge); 51 Todd Eberle; 52-53 Paul Ryan/International Interiors (Ina Garten); 54 above Hotze Eisma; 54 below John Hall; 55 Richard Waite; 56 C. Simon Sykes/The Interior Archive; 57 left Richard Felber; 57 right Ianthe Ruthven (Architect/ owners: Nicholas Groves-Raines & Kristin Hannesdottir); 58-59 John Miller; 59 right Fritz von der Schulenburg/The Interior Archive (Ann Vincent); 60-61 Ianthe Ruthven (Gene Garthwaite); 61 right Michael Mundy (Greg Munoz); 62 Ianthe Ruthven; 63 John Hall; 64 left David George; 64-65 Lars Hallen; 65 right Michael Mundy/Greg Munoz; 66 left Paul Ryan/International Interiors (Gerry Nelissen); 66-67 Paul Ryan/International Interiors (Gerry Nelissen); 68 Paul Ryan/International Interiors (John Saladion/Casdin); 69 above Jean-Pierre Godeaut (Maison Maurice); 69 below Simon McBride; 70-71 Rodney Hyett/Australian House & Garden Design Magazine; 70 above Ianthe Ruthven; 71 right Simon Brown/The Interior Archive; 72-73 C. Simon Sykes/The Interior Archive (Nicky Haslam); 72 left Ianthe Ruthven; 73 below Todd Eberle; 73 above Mads Mogensen; 74 above Richard Waite; 74 below Richard Waite; 75 right Nina Dreyer (Edvard Munch); 75 left Solvi Dos Santos; 76-77 Paul Ryan/International Interiors (Gertjan van der Host); 77 right Scott Frances/Esto; 78-79 Fritz von der Schulenburg/The Interior Archive; 80 below Tim Beddow/The Interior Archive; 80 above Simon McBride; 81 Ingalill Snitt; 82 John Hall; 83 Hotze Eisma (McCabe); 84-85 John Hall; 85 right Solvi Dos Santos; 86 left Hotze Eisma; 86 right Ianthe Ruthven; 87 Jean-Francois Jaussaud; 88 above John Miller; 88-89 Paul Ryan/International Interiors (D. & V. Tsingaris); 89 below Paul Ryan/International Interiors (D. & V. Tsingaris); 90-91 Nina Dreyer; 91 right Richard Waite; 92 Richard Felber; 93 Paul Ryan/International Interiors (John Saladion/Casdin); 94-95 Kari Haavisto; 94 left Solvi Dos Santos; 95 right Hotze Eisma (Boek, Netherlands); 96 Ianthe Ruthven (Architect/owners: Nicholas Groves-Raines & Kristin Hannesdottir); 97 below Hotze Eisma; 97 above Ingalill Snitt; 98-99 Simon McBride; 98 left Paul Ryan/International Interiors (Lee Mindel); 99 right Richard Felber; 100 left Fritz von der Schulenburg/The Interior Archive (Dot Spikings); 100-101 Jessie Walker; 101 right Richard Felber; 102 Solvi Dos Santos; 103 right Hotze Eisma; 103 left Jessie Walker; 104-105 Simon McBride (K. Brown); 104 left Gilles de Chabaneix (Stylist: Catherine Ardouin)/Marie Claire Maison; 105 right Alexandre Bailhache (Stylist: Catherine Ardouin)/Marie Claire Maison; 106 below Michael Mundy; 106 above Louzon/Stylograph (Stylist: C. D'Avella); 107 above Fritz von der Schulenburg/The Interior Archive (Francesco Miana d'Angoris); 107 below C. Simon Sykes/The Interior Archive; 108-109 Paul Ryan/International Interiors (Jo Naham); 108 right Solvi Dos Santos; 110-111 Solvi Dos Santos; 112 left Kari Haavisto; 112 right Eric Morin; 113 Gilles de Chabaneix (Stylist: Daniel Rozensztroch) /Marie Claire Maison; 114 John Hall; 115 Simon McBride; 116-117 Mark Darley/Esto; 116 left John Miller; 117 right Simon McBride; 118 above Hotze Eisma; 118 below and 119 Solvi Dos Santos; 120-121 Peter Woloszynski/The Interior Archive; 120 left C. Simon Sykes/The Interior Archive; 121 right Fritz von der Schulenburg/The Interior Archive; 122-123 Solvi Dos Santos 123 right Marie Pierre Morel (Stylist: Catherine Ardouin)/Marie Claire Maison; 124-125 Simon McBride; 124 left John Miller; 126-127 John Miller; 126 left Paul Ryan/International Interiors; 127 right Hamish Park/Insight Picture Library; 128-129 Hotze Eisma; 128 below Solvi Dos Santos; 129 right Richard Waite; 130 Hotze Eisma/Ariadne; 131 Fritz von der Schulenburg/The Interior Archive; 132-133 Hotze Eisma; 132 left Marianne Majerus; 134-135 Annet Held/Arcaid; 134 left Fritz von der Schulenburg/The Interior Archive (Emma Bini); 136 left Greg Powlesland; 136-137 Greg Powlesland; 137 left below Fritz von der Schulenburg/The Interior Archive; 137 right Ingalill Snitt; 137 right above Ingalill Snitt; 138-139 Mayer/Le Scanff /The Garden Picture Library; 138 centre Hamish Park/Insight Picture Library; 138 left Juliette Wade (Shucklets, Oxon); 139 right Richard Felber; 140 Nina Dreyer; 141 C. Simon Sykes/The Interior Archive.